CW01654520

If this book helps you in any way, please leave a review on Amazon. Every review helps other people to discover the book.

If you think a section in this book needs changing or updating, please email the author: chris@anachronistic.co.uk

With thanks to Rachel for her help,
support and love.

Copyright 2023 By Chris Darkin
All rights reserved. This book or any portion thereof may not be reproduced or used in any manner whatsoever without the express written permission of the publisher except for the use of brief quotations in a book review.
First printing 2022
Contact chris@anachronistic.co.uk

Contents

Part I

Introduction

So you've come (or are coming) to the conclusion that you don't believe in a god.

You may be in a situation where it is difficult to explore what this means for you. You may be part of a family, or community, or a nation where religion dominates. You may be surrounded by people with strong faiths, or be called upon to take part in practices you no longer feel you want to be part of.

A lack of belief can be challenging for some of the people around you. It may be greeted with concern, disappointment, misunderstanding, or anger.

You may feel isolated, or even persecuted, or you may feel the need to keep your doubts from the people you care about the most.

It may be difficult, confusing or infuriating – even if the people around you believe they are acting out of love and compassion. The simple fact of being surrounded by a worldview you are questioning can make you feel isolated, and alone.

This book is intended as a survival guide for the non-believer in a faith-filled world.

Perhaps you've always had doubts, but you no longer feel you can ignore them. Perhaps you've only recently started re-examining the foundations of the beliefs of those around you, and are now wondering what this means for your relationships, your identity and your values.

Either way, you've done an amazing thing already. You've managed to look outside the constraints of the ideas around you, and come to a different view on your own.

That's brave, thoughtful, and worthy.

You may want to begin by turning to the blank pages in the back of this book and listing anything you are worried about: any relationships you are concerned may suffer; any fears about making sense of life, any worries about the effect on your life, or your plans for the future; and any difficulties you see in exploring the questions you feel you need to ask. Putting these into words may help you tackle them.

It might also help you make a distinction between the questions you need to ask yourself, and the consequences you fear the answers will have for you.

It's important to give yourself the space and time to think critically. Being surrounded by people who all have the same worldview can make it hard to think outside that worldview. Likewise, religious practice has been fine-tuned over thousands of years to reinforce feelings of belonging, and community, and to create the emotional connection that people feel as a sincere relationship with God.

It is astonishing how much we are all affected by the mood and behaviour of those around us. A contemporary religious service is a textbook example of psychological conditioning and group bonding techniques.

These techniques can include: Being required to affirm your belief out loud as part of a group, in front of a group, or alone; continual repetition of important phrases and lessons; singing or chanting together in a group; being encouraged to restrict your thoughts on certain subjects; being encouraged to share or confess deeply personal feelings or thoughts; repeated routines like prayer, churchgoing, or rituals; and inclusion of religious worship and symbols in every part of your life.

You may find you need to step away, when you are permitted to, from some of these influences, in order to allow yourself to think more clearly.

A final note:

This book is not about debunking any particular faith.
It does come from an atheist perspective and it offers defences to common religious arguments, but these aren't about saying that (for example) the Christian God definitely doesn't exist, only that the evidence presented to say that it does has alternative explanations. The arguments in this book don't pretend to deny the possibility of a god (I'm using a small "g" here as there are many possible gods in which people believe). They simply suggest ways in which the arguments usually given to prove gods are real aren't up to the job.

YOU ARE NOT ALONE

It's tricky to measure who believes what. There can be serious consequences for saying you don't agree with the majority in your country (non-believers are persecuted in some countries, believers are persecuted in others).

However, surveys suggest up to 39% of Americans and 69% of British people don't believe in any gods. The rest of the world varies, but there are non-believers everywhere, and that number is rising every year.

Not every one of them is a campaigner. Most are simply living quietly honest and ethical lives all around the world without a god.

Even if you are part of a community which is steeped in religion, the chances are you already know people who quietly do not believe, or who have doubts but keep them to themselves.

If you feel isolated, search online and you'll find some excellent non-faith bloggers and voices on YouTube.

IT IS OK TO GRIEVE

Losing your faith is like a bereavement or a divorce. Perhaps you were a committed believer or perhaps you only ever followed the beliefs of those around you. Either way, if religion has been a big part of your life, parting company from it can feel like a heavy loss.

An important relationship is ending – and this feeling is real even if you now believe that relationship was only ever in your own mind.

Even if the rational part of you has let go of beliefs, you may have a lifetime of behaviours and ways of thinking that the emotional part of you will be slower to let go of.

It's ok if you still find yourself talking to a god you don't believe in, or yearning for the feeling of purpose and meaning. It's natural to feel alone or abandoned, to experience loss, and to wonder how you will cope with making decisions and finding your way.

Many ex-believers struggle with guilt or fear or sadness as hangovers from their old religions long after they have come to the logical conclusion that their fears are unfounded. Children fear monsters under their beds long after they know there are no monsters. If you fear the wrath of a god you don't believe in, don't worry. It is just an emotional echo.

Allow yourself to grieve what you have lost. You are not being unreasonable.

YOUR PAST WAS NOT WASTED

Just because you've changed your mind about faith, does not mean everything you learned in the past is wrong. Neither does it mean that you are not the person you were before, or that you have wasted that part of your life.

Think of it this way: If you don't believe in a god, then all those things you previously felt were given to you by your god – your resilience in difficult times, your strength of character, your courage in making difficult decisions, your morality, and your achievements – all these things were you. You made those decisions alone. You found the strength from yourself. You showed your own moral courage.

If your god wasn't real, then you must have created them in your image. You haven't lost those strengths, you've just claimed them as your own.

You are the same person you always were, and everything you ever did is still valid.

IT'S OK TO ASK ANY QUESTION

No questions are forbidden.

You may have been discouraged from asking certain questions in the past. You may have felt that exploration of ideas which contradicted the faith of those around you was shut-down, ridiculed, or ignored.

No such restrictions exist when you are a non-believer. You can ask anything, be interested in anything, challenge any idea – including the idea of non-belief.

You can follow whatever train of thought you want to, and reach whatever conclusions you like.

Nobody is looking over your shoulder. Nobody will disapprove.

AND YOU CAN

FIND

ANSWERS ANYWHERE

You may be used to the idea that answers to important questions must all come back to one set of teachings, or holy book.

You may feel lost once you start to doubt whether those teachings are infallible. You may wonder where your answers will come from.

For non-believers, answers are wherever you find them. Look in the holy books. Look in the science books. Look on YouTube, or Wikipedia, or in your favourite fiction. Listen to your friends and your enemies.

All that matters is that you sharpen your critical thinking skills and learn to see the strengths and weaknesses of the answers you find.

And remember, none of the answers you find is final. All are subject to change when better information comes along.

YOU DON'T HAVE TO

KNOW ALL THE ANSWERS

You don't have to know everything.

Being unhappy with the answers you've been given is enough.

That's one of the best things about not being religious. There's no pressure to pretend you know the answers to questions about life, or that those questions even have single answers. If you don't know something, you can say you don't know.

Replacing religious certainty with scientific certainty isn't the point. "I don't know" is a powerful answer and not having to pretend you have all the answers when you don't is very empowering.

To be clear, when talking to theists, you may need to add "I don't believe anyone else knows either" as people are often scared by uncertainty or interpret it as weakness of argument. They often leap in with the answers their faith has given them.

But it is fine, absolutely fine, not to know the answers to important questions.

Science is not about being certain about answers. It constantly updates itself as more is learned about the universe.

The search for truth is the search for better questions.

YOU DON'T HAVE TO

GO TO CHURCH

SING

PRAY

OR TAKE PART IN

RELIGIOUS LIFE

People close to you may try to encourage you to go to church, or take part in religious events even when they know you don't want to. This may be uncomfortable if you don't believe, particularly if your reasons lead you to question the ethical values of your religion.

There may be regular worship, or religious study that does not feel right for you anymore. There may be prayers or singing at the dinner table, at school, or at your workplace. It may feel like you are being hypercritical by continuing to join in, but at the same time, that refusing to do so would mark you out for unwanted attention.

It may be that you feel you should make the point that you do not believe by refusing to be part of rituals or groups you no longer see any sense in, but you may fear the effect of this on others' opinions of you.

There may be subtle emotional pressure, or peer pressure. There may be attempts to make you feel guilty, and you may feel you are letting other people down by not attending, not joining in. You may feel there will be a fight if you don't do certain things or behave in certain ways.

People may be acting out of what they see as your best interest. However, it is ok to firmly, but politely, decline to do anything you don't feel comfortable with.

Remember, nobody has the right to tell you what to believe.

YOU DON'T HAVE TO

STOP GOING TO CHURCH

Once they decide they do not believe in a god, many people want to stay far away from religious spaces. It may be that there are bad memories there, or people whose attention is toxic.

However, you may find the rituals, the singing, the aesthetic of religion comforting in itself. You may decide that religious community still has value to you and others.

You don't have to stop going. If you want to be part of a choir, or enjoy the social aspect of a church, that's fine. You don't need to believe to do that.

If it works for you, do it.

If it's not the right time to tell people around you, then go along with it. If there's no God, then you're not upsetting anyone.

There are plenty of churchgoers, and even leaders in every religion, for whom the ethical or community side of church is far more important than belief in particular gods or dogmas.

Be on the lookout for others who may feel the same, and find common cause with them.

MORALITY
DOESN'T COME FROM
RELIGION

Humans were making ethical decisions for a good million years or so before the gods people worship now were invented. That's how society evolved. A social species like ours needed to learn to be good to each other to survive.

In the past, religion did a lot of work developing our ethical ideas into stories and sets of rules, and guides which helped to structure ancient civilisations. Rules like some of the Ten Commandments were helpful in their time.

That said, religion didn't invent those ideas. Humans' objections to killing and stealing didn't begin on stone tablets, and religions don't have copyright on them now. Morality has moved on since holy books were written, and we've learned a lot more about humanity, psychology, philosophy, and the natural world.

It's natural, then, that our views of ethics have become more sophisticated.

Your ethical views might include some you've learned from religion, and others you've learned elsewhere, or developed yourself.

And that's fine.

Religion doesn't own morality.

YOU DON'T HAVE TO

LET OTHERS DEFINE YOUR ATHEISM

When you tell someone you're a non-believer, they may have all kinds of preconceptions about what that means.

They may try to project those ideas onto you.

Not believing in a god or gods means just that. It doesn't imply anything else. You might have a whole worldview surrounding your lack of belief, but any conversation that starts off with "if you don't believe in God then you must believe this…" should set off all kinds of warning bells.

In particular, the idea that an atheist has to either fervently believe that there is no spiritual dimension to life, or that they have to demonstrate unquestioning commitment to some other dogma, is simply untrue.

Neither do they have to prove to everyone they meet that god isn't real.

If I claim to have magical powers, you don't have to be able to prove I don't. You just have to wait for me to show you my tricks.

YOU DON'T HAVE TO CONVINCE YOUR FRIENDS & FAMILY

It's tempting to want to share new ideas with those around you.

It's easy to feel that if only you could explain how you came to your views, then they'd understand.

Unfortunately that probably won't happen.

By all means, try your best to get people to understand where you're coming from. However, know that they may not be at the same point as you.

Even if they have thought some of the same things as you, and are asking similar questions, they may not be ready to explore their conclusions.

You may have to explore your non-belief away from those who are closest to you.

Later, they may be ready to understand your point of view, but that may take months, or years. For now, you might need to agree to disagree – or even stay away from talking about sensitive questions. Above all, stay calm.

YOU DON'T HAVE TO EXPLAIN YOUR NON-BELIEF

The people who love you may feel betrayed.

They may feel they need bring you back into the fold.

They may feel eager to make sure you share every step of your journey with them.

You don't have to do that.

You don't have to explain every doubt you've had or every new question you've asked yourself, or every new perspective you've seen – and you especially don't have to do this around people who, however well-meaning, have an interest in extinguishing independent curiosity.

If you feel you need to become better informed about the questions you're asking, or that you just need to think about them some more before approaching church leaders, or loved ones with your half-formed ideas, that's fine.

Give yourself that time.

You don't need to give a running commentary on your internal struggles. If you want to say something, you can just say that the old explanations aren't convincing to you anymore.

YOU DON'T HAVE TO
REPLACE
OLD DOGMAS
WITH
NEW DOGMAS

It's very easy to feel cut adrift when you abandon an old set of rules. It can call into question everything about your way of life.

When this happens, it's tempting to grab onto a new set of rules and apply them to yourself in the same rigid way as you have before.

But you don't have to. Remember, what you're giving up is not a god – not if you don't believe in one.

What you're giving up is the *idea* of infallibility.

No leader, no book, no set of ideas are always right.

YOU DON'T HAVE TO

PROVE GOD

IS NOT

REAL

Saying you don't believe a god or gods exist is not the same as claiming that you know they don't.

You don't have to be able to prove there's no god. That's not your job. You can give it a go, if you feel strongly, but you don't have to.

It's up to those who believe to provide the evidence. It's not up to you. A Christian doesn't have to prove that Zeus and Thor aren't real, so it's not up to a non-believer to prove that any gods are made up.

All that most non-believers are saying is that they haven't seen convincing evidence, and so until they do, they'll behave just the same way to all humankind's invented gods: Zeus, Thor, Allah, and the many versions of the Christian god.

Most atheists aren't claiming proof that gods don't exist, they're just putting them all in the same basket of equally improbable things until better evidence comes along.

STILL OK TO BE ANGRY

You may be angry or concerned at the power religion continues to have in society, politics, or more locally over your life and the lives of those around you.

Religion has done some pretty bad things – from the Crusades to slavery to the massacres of unbelievers throughout history. There are countless acts of terrorism, war and genocide that can be blamed on faith. On top of that, there is injustice caused by discrimination against women, against homosexuals, and against other faiths. There are multiple and continuing cases of individual and collective abuses of power, physical, mental and sexual abuse, and there is suffering and death caused by outdated attitudes to contraception, medicine, and mental health.

Religion likes to put these things down to a few bad apples, but the bad things just keep coming, and institutions continue to fail to deal with them.

Religion may have done bad things to you or those you love. You may feel it has affected your family, your mental health, or caused guilt over perceived sins (especially sexual ones). If this makes you angry, that's fine. You have every right.

Anger has a place: if you've ever been bullied or threatened, you'll know that showing anger can be the only way to stop an immediate danger to yourself or others, or to make someone understand the harm they are doing to you.

BUT

YOU DON'T HAVE TO BE

ANGRY

ALL THE TIME

Being angry with someone continually never made them your friend.

And like it or not, religion is going to be around for a while. We have to get on with those we disagree with.

We have to find ways of reaching out, of finding common ground.

Your local church may be preaching intolerance towards same-sex couples, but at the same time, it may be raising money for refugees. It may be condoning discrimination, but at the same time, looking after the old, the sick and the poor.

It's a complex landscape, and you cannot navigate it with anger alone.

YOU CAN ALWAYS CHANGE YOUR MIND

Certainty is the enemy.

You wouldn't expect to come out of school with the same understanding of the world you went in with. You'd expect to learn and grow.

If you don't believe in a god or gods, that's fine.

If you learn some more, and find a different worldview that's fine too.

If you doubt your doubts and return to your original faith, or get a new one, that's ok.

You can change your mind as often as you like about whatever you like, and you can do it for whatever reason you feel makes sense.

Changing your mind is a sign that you're growing and learning.

If you feel like your world view is getting claustrophobic, take a vacation from it and learn a new perspective. You can always go back.

Whatever helps you to learn more is good.

YOU DON'T HAVE TO

FEAR

THE WRATH OF

GODS

OR THE DECEPTION OF

DEVILS

This may seem obvious but without a god, nobody is going to reward you for doing the right thing. Nobody is going to punish you for doing the wrong thing.

Nobody is even going to tell you which is which. Sure, people will try, but they're just people, and they're all fallible.

God is not out there pointing you in the right direction, nor are there devils trying to lead you down the wrong path.

It's quite simply up to you to decide what is good, and it's up to you to do it, not out of fear, or hope of reward, but simply because you are a good person who is driven by love, empathy and compassion.

YOU
ARE
A GOOD
PERSON

How do you know that you're a good person?

Because you're evolved to be. If you don't believe in a god, then there's no place for the idea of Original Sin.

Sure you might have flaws, some of your evolution encourages you to do bad things. Also your evolution was pretty good for the African plains where your species evolved, but we're in a more complex world now, so the waters are muddied and ethics needs a bit more thought than it did when we just had to decide how to share out the fruit we'd picked.

That said, we can point to the way society has grown and evolved to become better over the centuries. That's all down to humans.

And remember all those brilliant lessons on how to live well that you see in religious books? If you don't believe in a god or gods, then they're all created by humans - brilliant, ethical humans struggling to make the world a fairer place than it was when we scavenged for food on the African savanna.

Humans like you.

YOU ARE HONESTLY SEEKING TRUTH

A lot of the questions aimed at non-believers are centred around accusations of dishonesty, or insincerity.

Examples include:

"You're denying God", "You're betraying your faith", "You're being deceived", "You just want to sin without repercussions".

It's easy to see why. To someone who embraces their religion wholeheartedly, it is the centre of who they are and their experience of the world. To know that someone else experiences the same world and comes to different conclusions can be threatening, confusing and hard to believe.

Be assured that the fact that you're asking questions and the fact that you're reading this book means you are trying to understand the world better.

And that, in the end, is all anyone can ask of you.

YOU DON'T HAVE TO
WIN EVERY ARGUMENT

You're just starting to explore what non-belief means to you. Religion, meanwhile, has had thousands of years to develop and fine-tune techniques to defend its point of view.

In addition, individuals within religion are often honest, intelligent and thoughtful people who have dedicated themselves to the study of their beliefs, and who spend their time arguing about their faith.

They often know their subject and are eloquent and powerful speakers.

They may come up with points you haven't thought of, or new twists on old arguments that you'll need to take away, and spend some time unpacking.

They may even come up with evidence that you need to go away and check out before you can explore it.

There's a space in the back of this book to note down anything you discover that needs further study, or any arguments that you feel are powerful – especially if they contradict your own feelings.

You are, after all, on an honest search for truth.

YOU CAN STILL

CELEBRATE CHRISTMAS

EASTER

DIWALI

RAMADAN

The festivals we now call Christmas and Easter were being celebrated long before Jesus was supposed to have existed.

They were appropriated by the Christian church as a way to sell the idea of Jesus to pagans. Recently, the celebrations have come to mean very different things to different people all around the world. Plenty of non-religious people celebrate Christmas as a time for family and friends. Plenty of others have preferred to leave religiously inspired festivals behind. It's completely up to you.

Feasting around a decorated tree in your living room while a man in a flying sleigh delivers presents isn't any more or less strange when you add or remove a magic baby from the proceedings. If it works for you, it's all good.

The same goes for all feasts, celebrations and religious practices. You can take what is meaningful for you from them and leave what isn't.

YOU DON'T HAVE TO THROW AWAY YOUR BIBLE

You might decide that you don't want to give up the social and emotional benefits of belonging to a community, or the calming benefits of the rhythm of ritual, prayer or worship. It may feel as it it's all or nothing, but many people hold agnostic or liberal beliefs rather than more fundamentalist or literal ones. They may be comfortable with the idea that a holy book contains many inspiring and helpful stories and metaphors but accept that it was written in a particular cultural context and therefore has some outdated ideas. It can be difficult to make that leap when you have been taught that complete trust in the literal truth of your holy book is essential to your salvation or fate after death and an indication of your loyalty. But many people have made that leap from certainty to ambiguity. Even believers in a literal interpretation of, for example, the Bible accept some parts as metaphor or poetry, such as the sun moving across the sky in Psalm 19 (which was used to censor Galileo's findings about the Earth going round the sun); or God as both father and mother.

There are plenty of churches and other religious communities that are relaxed the exact nature of your beliefs.

You might decide to say something like "I benefit from my experiences of something that I don't need to justify the existence of" or "I have a relationship with a being that may or may not exist". You can also say "I am comfortable with being on a journey and I don't need to have all the answers" or "There may or may not be something beyond the physical world, but I don't need to pin down all the details."

Part II

Interactions with believers

If you don't believe in a god, and you're in a situation in which others do, then sooner or later, you're going to end up discussing it.

You may do your best to avoid this kind of conversation, or you may seek it out. Either way, it's good to know what arguments and challenges are likely to be presented to you, and be prepared for how you'll respond.

Good quality dialogue between people of faith and non-believers is important, but it can be difficult. Often believers are attempting to convert you, or put pressure on you (even if they don't realise that's what they're doing). Often, belief is at the centre of the being of the person you're talking to, and you'll need to be sensitive to the fact that your mere existence as a compassionate, intelligent atheist may be challenging to their understanding of the world.

You may be seen as a threat, or as a victim, or as an aggressor, and they may take any of those roles in response.

To make matters more complex, it may be that the first people you have these discussions with will be those closest to you – your friends, your family, people with power, and people you respect.

Most will believe they know what's best for you, and many will have preconceptions and misunderstandings about what your lack of belief means.

This section includes a few of the most commonly put questions and challenges to non-believers. It's likely you'll have to answer many of them multiple times, in a variety of different forms.

This book can't tell you how to answer. That will depend on your own journey and worldview, but it tries to give a few pointers about what is behind the questions, and how you can begin to approach them.

Before you enter a conversation about faith, it's important to know what you're trying to achieve.

Success does not mean presenting the person you're talking to with a question they can't answer, or humiliating them, or dismantling their faith for them.

Often, the aim is simply to get the other person to realise that you are both on an honest search for truth, or that you have thought about your point of view as much as they have about theirs.

Often, success simply means dispelling a misconception, or making sure that you, or your questioner, asks better questions in the future.

Sometimes, it is enough to convince your companion that while you share some common ground, you will not be easily dissuaded from continuing to ask difficult questions even if this means your relationship has to change.

Whatever your aims, however, you can always try to listen and understand others' viewpoints, while at the same time, being as clear about yours as you can.

Stay calm, and show that you're comfortable and at peace with your new self.

Be thoughtful, be compassionate, and be respectful. After all, that is what you want from the person you're talking to.

Finally, if someone asks you a question you struggle to answer, or puts a point that strikes a chord with you, remember it. Try writing it down at the back of this book, and think about it, or research it later on.

If you think it needs including in this book, please email chris@anachronistic.co.uk and I'll try to add it in.

"There's only one true faith."

The first commandment: "Thou shalt have no other god than me" has got a lot to answer for here. It has been used to justify persecution, murder, and religious war on such a scale that it could be argued to be the single most damaging statement anybody has ever made.

But let's have a little humility. Not many people will say so, but everyone thinks their belief system is superior to those of other people. You'd have to feel that way, or you'd change your belief system, right?

For many, however, not believing in any gods means there's no "one true answer". There are just changing shades of doubt which adapt themselves as we learn more. It's a difficult message to get across to someone who has the security of certainty.

So how do you argue with someone who flat out states that there's only one answer and it's theirs?

You might try to get them to explain what is special about their religion. Why it is different from the thousands of other religions, sects and churches out there, and why only the very few members of that church are the only people to whom truth has been revealed. The reasons you get back will be enlightening, but often circular (If, for example, you don't already believe Jesus was the son of God, then the idea that he started the Catholic church won't cut much ice).

“All religions are just attempts to describe the same thing.”

This is the opposite of the "one true faith" argument.

It's more open and thoughtful, and does accept that nobody has all the answers to important questions. A discussion with someone who has this view is likely to be fruitful and understanding.

Many non believers would probably agree with it as stated here.

A scientific approach to this theory might be to try to strip away all the things that make one religion different from others in an attempt to isolate exactly what they have in common, and so learn more about what it is they're trying to describe.

Many non-believers would suggest that once you found the similarities, what would be left would be simply a tendency in humans to search for patterns where there are mysteries, to turn them into stories, and to use music, and ritual to reinforce the feeling of community and security within groups. In other words, a survival mechanism which would have served our ancestors well as we evolved, but which is less useful in navigating complex scientific and ethical choices today.

“But the Bible says…”

You can't use a holy book to prove itself.

If I wrote in a book "everything in this book is true" and then, when that was challenged, I said "but look, it says it here in the book that it's true, so it must be," would that be evidence?

It's fine to use examples from a holy book to illustrate ideas and concepts (i.e using the Bible's description of Noah to illustrate faith), but that's not the same as proof (i.e. using it to claim that Noah's flood was a real event). You need a source from somewhere else to back up every claim. Be clear when someone is using a quote as an illustration, and when they're trying to pass it off as evidence.

Every line in any book needs proving on its own and independently of the book.

It may be worth pointing out that if you don't believe the Bible is literally true, then quoting from it isn't the way to convince you that it is.

"Mine is the only God because..."

Everything you can say about your god is also true of a thousand others.

Theists often list the unique parts of their own faith – for example, the resurrection – which is fine, if they think theirs is the only faith ever to have that feature, and think it's important.

However, every faith has unique aspects, whether it's their prophets, or their gods, or some aspect of their philosophies. It's not enough to be different. Those differences have to amount to evidence otherwise, they're just statements that you believe in this philosophy, or that prophet, or some facet of a particular god.

In the end, the only thing that can make a faith "the one true faith" is if every single claim it makes can be demonstrated to be true.

“What if you’re wrong?”

This argument is called Pascal's Wager. The idea is that if there is no god, then not believing in one gains you nothing. You still die.

If, however, there is a god (and it happens to be the god of whoever you're talking to) then the non-believer will lose any hope of salvation and be condemned forever.

So, the argument goes, you may as well believe because you stand to gain eternal life if it turns out there's a god.

The problem with this argument is that you can apply it to any god you like. What if you're wrong about Zeus? Or Thor? What if you're worshipping the wrong God?

Pascal's Wager is only an argument from the point of view of someone who already believes – because, for them, there are only two options: believing in their god and not believing in their god. The difficulty is to persuade them that you see their god as just one of the ten thousand or so deities humanity has produced.

“Prove that God isn’t real.”

The idea of this question is to make it your job to prove whether or not God exists.

But it isn't your job.

If you believe in a god, and you want to convince someone who doesn't then it's up to you to stump up the proof. Non-believers don't have to prove anything.

Being an atheist or an agnostic doesn't mean believing that there is no god. It means simply *not* having seen evidence that there *is* one. It's not a belief, it's a lack of belief.

Once your questioner understands this, they will realise that providing evidence is the only way to convince you.

"I have a meaningful, loving relationship with my God and it's real to me. Are you denying that?"

This statement is just someone saying that their faith has helped them in some way. This is great, and few atheists would want to deny them that.

Lots of people feel religion has got them through difficult times. Others swear by the value of meditation. Some get immense feelings of identity from football, or draw life lessons from Star Wars. It's fine, it really is.

And it's fine for Star Wars fans to try to convince you to give Star Wars a go.

But there's a difference between "real to me" and "real". Someone's relationship with their god may be a reason for them to have faith, and want to tell you about it. But it isn't proof that the relationship exists outside of their mind. It's worth noting here that imagining someone loves you has the same effect on your body as being loved by a real person.

Feeling love doesn't prove that person exists, but it does have similar benefits.

The fact that someone gains insight or resilience, or anything else from something doesn't mean you will too.

If you don't feel the same about Star Wars that someone else does, that doesn't negate their love for the franchise. They can try to push you to share their love, but they must expect you to respond with your criticisms, and if you think the story is absurd, they shouldn't be offended when you say so.

"Science just explains *how* the universe works.

You need God to explain *why*."

Not all questions require an answer.

There may not be an answer to "why" the universe exists. You can explain how a mountain came to be, but the question: "what is the point of a mountain?" is meaningless.

This point is often made in order to say that science and religion are not in opposition, but simply answer different questions.

You may believe this. You may not.

However, the logical conclusion of it is to argue for a god which obeys the rules of physics (either because they're constrained by them, or because they've chosen to run the universe according to those rules – like a clockwork toy).

If a god ever breaks the rules of physics to (for example) perform miracles, then those miracles should be observable and testable by science – because the laws of physics won't always work. This has never been observed.

However, if the god never breaks those laws, then worship is pointless. A god which acts only according to the rules of physics cannot respond to prayer, or send prophets, or perform miracles or, indeed do anything.

You may ask what's the practical difference between that god and no god at all?

“In the Big Bang, what exploded?”

This is a great question. It's something scientists have been wrestling with for years, and nobody really knows.

The phrase, Big Bang is just used to describe the fact that we've seen that everything in the universe is moving away from everything else, and getting cooler.

This means, unless some change has happened to the universe, there was a time, way back, when everything was much closer together and much hotter. Simple as that. This doesn't tell us what happened before. However, not knowing doesn't mean we can jump straight to assuming some guy did it. That would raise more questions than it answered.

What your questioner is getting at here is that science depends on the law of cause and effect. But, surely, if you go back far enough you'll eventually have to kick off existence with an effect (the universe) that has no cause.

It's a decent question, but not one to which a god is a good answer. We don't even know what *time* is, so it may make little sense to talk about "the beginning" of everything.

In short, there are dozens of theories that don't require a "beginning" or an "uncaused event". We've a lot more work to do before we can answer that question, and just dropping a god in as a hypothesis has turned out to be the wrong solution every time anyone's tried it in the past.

Arguing that because we don't know something, the answer must be a god just isn't good logic.

“Why is there something rather than nothing?”

This is a similar question to the Big Bang question. And it's a brilliant one. Why is there a universe?

Nobody has a good answer. Not science, not religion, not philosophy, not even fiction has managed a satisfying answer to this question. People have been arguing about it for millennia.

The problem is that our whole experience is limited within our universe. It's impossible to imagine what it would be like if there were no universe - none of the physical laws that we experience, no light, no matter, no time.

It's equally difficult to see how that state of affairs – whatever it was, or is – could give rise to everything we see around us.

The temptation to speculate is irresistible. You're probably doing it right now.

The trouble is, our speculations are only fed by what we can imagine, so we fill the mystery with gods which look, speak and behave like ourselves, and which have morals, needs, and plans of which we approve.

Our ideas about the mysteries of the universe are fascinating and wonderful. They may even become useful or accurate in the far future. Right now, we have to work hard to keep our beautiful and beguiling speculations from hardening into unsupported beliefs.

"If there is a cause behind the finite universe, wouldn't that have to be infinite?"

Nope, I can be the cause of finite things, and I'm pretty finite myself. If something created the universe, it could easily have been more finite than the universe.

There's no more reason to imagine an infinite creator for the universe than to think that a seed has to be bigger than a tree.

“If there was a creator, it must have been my god.”

Of course, nobody actually says this, but it's an underlying assumption for every religious conversation about the creation of the universe.

And there's a problem with that because it's a huge leap from wondering if the universe has some kind of conscious creator to wholehearted adoption of one particular version of one particular god. Even if you could prove that the universe was a deliberate, conscious creation:

It could have been a version of the Christian God
It could have been Allah,
Or Odin, or Zeus.
Perhaps it was an evil god
Or an imperfect god
Or a thousand gods working together
Or a committee
Or a machine
Or a human from the future
Or a mad god, or a stupid one
It could have been a god who subsequently died
Or has no interest in humans
Or created no afterlife
Or is subservient to its own rules
Ours could have been a test for a better universe
Or perhaps it was built for another species
Or our descendants
Maybe the universe itself is conscious
Or is a simulation
Or the creator is something we can't even imagine
Or maybe one of a million other possibilities…
Or maybe nothing.

"Can an effect be greater than its cause? – can you give what you don't have?"

Certainly you can give what you don't have. Anyone who has children knows that they grow up to have attributes and abilities neither of their parents had. If that weren't the case, we'd all be less than our parents.

This question is actually framed to suggest that whatever created the universe must be greater than the universe.

However, it doesn't define what "greater" means in this sense. Does it mean bigger? More intelligent? Does it mean it must have more things in it? Or does it just mean 'older'?

An avalanche is certainly greater, in most respects, than the snowball required to set it off, so there's a small cause with a big effect.

A good religious apologist's response to this is that an avalanche doesn't just need a snowball, it needs snow, a mountain, a weather system, etc.

However, there's no easy way to transfer that metaphor to talking about the universe. We can't make any reliable statements about what was required to produce the universe. We don't know what the "weather" was like back then, so we can't make any deductions about the "snowball".

“How come the universe is even suitable for life?”

This is a good one. It's called the teleological argument.

If the rules of the universe were even slightly different from how they are, we can't imagine how life could evolve. Surely that means those rules must have been set up this way – otherwise we're a billion to one chance.

Good point.

Except, we have no idea about the conditions under which the universe came to be, so we can't make any judgements about what is likely or unlikely about its make-up. It may be there was no other possible way for physics to be. Maybe there are or were a trillion other failed universes with no life. Maybe life of some kind would have showed up whatever the rules of the universe were – if, as many believe, life is a natural consequence of complexity.

All we know for sure is that we're here, and the life we see has emerged to take advantage of the laws of physics that exist in this universe.

Again, substituting "we don't know" for "a god did it" isn't a leap many are willing to make. Even if it were, there are 10,000 gods to pick from, and no reason to think any of them were around before mankind started worshiping them.

“Doesn’t an intelligently designed universe need an intelligent designer?”

It's not an intelligently designed universe.

It's a really badly designed universe in lots of ways (depending obviously on what, if anything, you think it was designed for).

You can think of the universe as a kind of sorting process. Anything that's thrown up by the random churn of events, like collapsing or exploding stars, either survives or doesn't. We're now thirteen billion years into that process, so all the randomly produced stuff that didn't make it has gone. This leaves us with a universe that seems to rub along for now in a relatively stable way.

Nothing intelligent about that.

You do have to wonder, though, if humans were supposed to be any significant part of creation, why an intelligent creator would have made it so inhospitable for us.

Why, if you were creating a universe as a home for human life "in your image", would you create a billion galaxies which humans could never hope to glimpse let alone visit? Why would you then play out that universe utterly devoid of humanity for thirteen billion years, only to introduce us just at the last second into a tiny world shoved off into an unimportant corner of the cosmos?

If this universe is intelligently designed, then the one thing we can be sure of is that it wasn't made with us in mind.

"If you found a watch, wouldn't you deduce that a watchmaker existed?"

This is just a rerun of the argument that the universe is complex, so it can't be accidental.

There's nothing wrong with this view. The universe is certainly complex and wonderful, and if you don't know how something works, it's easy to see it as spiritual.

Science is the attempt to understand that complexity, and it's come a very long way in a few centuries. We're now at the stage where certain large parts of the stunning complexity of the universe are clear – the way the stars were formed, how life evolved, why sunsets are colorful and how we experience those colors as beautiful.

Every year we learn more, and the one thing that comes up time and time again is that when we unravel the complexity of a part of the universe, we discover that no magic is required to make it work.

In all the equations so far discovered that describe how nature works, no gods have ever been needed.

"Why are there people (conscious beings) if the universe is just matter and energy?"

We don't know what consciousness is, so again, we can't make any assumptions about the answer to that.

"God did it" isn't any better answer to that than it is to the question "how does the sun move?" or "how do plants grow?". Both of these questions we put down to direct divine intervention in the past.

But the specific version of the question often put here is:

"How can you get consciousness from matter and energy? If matter isn't conscious, how can it become conscious?" In other words, how can something (matter) produce an attribute it doesn't contain (consciousness)?

Well, it does. Combining things produces new attributes. Happens all the time.

A match doesn't contain fire, but it can produce fire. Hydrogen and oxygen have none of the attributes of water, but they become water when you combine them.

“How do you know the Earth is millions of years old?”

About a dozen different ways:

We know how far away the stars are, so we can work out that light took millions of years to get here from them.

We know the speed the continents are moving apart, so we can work out how long ago they were joined.

We know the speed the radioactivity of carbon decays so we can work out how long ago it was formed.

We know the rate DNA mutates so we can work out how long various species have been around.

The point here is that all these are completely separate measures from unconnected fields of science. And yet they all come up with the same answer: the Earth is millions of years old.

The other explanation is that a god changed every grain of sand on every beach, moved the continents, altered the DNA of every creature, and changed the speed of light. And all with no other purpose than to lie to us.

That's a lot of work compared to the amount of work that went into – say – writing the bible.

So either the earth is millions of years old, or you believe in a god whose most obvious contribution to humanity was to lie to us.

"If we evolved from monkeys, why are there still monkeys?"

Monkeys didn't change into humans just as your parents didn't change into you. They gave birth to you. That's why your parents can still be around at the same time as you are.

"Why are there still monkeys?" is a poor quality argument.

If someone tries this on you, it's a pretty good indication that they've not thought for more than a couple of seconds about their viewpoint.

This doesn't make them dumb. It just means they don't really care about the proofs of evolution. That in itself should be a bit of a warning signal that you probably won't get far in your discussions.

Anyway....

Most people agree that dogs were bred from wolves (or relatives of wolves), but there are still wolves. Humans bred wolves, keeping those that showed the traits they wanted for (say) hunting, and, gradually wolves and dogs became separate, looking and behaving differently.

The ancestors of monkeys didn't, of course have people selecting their traits to make them more human-like. Some just took up lifestyles that took them down different evolutionary paths. A couple of million years later, here we are.

“We don’t know the origin of life.”

We kind of do.

We know how organic molecules formed. We can do it in a test tube. We know how the first single celled creatures appeared and evolved into multicellular life. We can follow the train of evolution through DNA and the fossil record right up to humanity. Sure, there are plenty of gaps, but they're getting smaller and smaller every year.

If you're going to pin your belief on our lack of knowledge about this, then you're standing on an iceberg that's shrinking year by year.

"Evolution is just a theory."

Yes.
So is gravity.
Stuff still falls when you drop it.

Theory in science doesn't just mean "unsubstantiated guess". A theory has to have a substantial body of evidence to back it up. Both evolution and gravity are incomplete theories – they're still being worked on and new things are being discovered about them. However, in terms of evidence, evolution is as well supported as gravity.

“How could we have come from a single cell?”

When we were conceived, we started off as a single cell, and that cell grew into us, so we know it's physically possible for a human to grow from a single cell.

We can also trace the evolution of how it happened using two different methods. We can do it through fossils – where we can show how worms became fish, fish became reptiles, reptiles became mammals and eventually us.

We can also show it through our DNA in which we can see patterns which we share with other creatures. These are patterns which created useful structures way back in previous creatures (like fins and gills) but which we don't use in our bodies.

We can even look at the embryos of our own species, and see that they are very similar to those of fish. They even have gill-slits.

Unless a god planted unused instructions to give our bodies gills that we never develop and never use, that information must have come from our ancestors.

“Evolution from one species to another has never been proved.”

The argument here is a defence against the fact that we can demonstrate evolution easily by simply breeding animals to bring out certain traits. Dogs, for example have been cross bred from wolves to create a whole series of variations. Farm animals, plants and other creatures obviously evolve and we can watch them doing it.

The argument here, though, is that however you breed a dog, it's still a dog. You'd never call it another species.

The problem with the argument is that the term "species" is one we've invented. It doesn't mean anything to nature itself. Obviously, a cat and a dog are different animals, but the exact line we draw between one species and another is just one we've come up with for our own convenience.

The best definition we have is that animals of different species are those which have become so different they can no longer breed naturally and produce fertile offspring. However, lions and tigers can do exactly that, so can brown bears and polar bears.

In other words, there's no difference in nature between evolution within species and evolution from one species to another. All that's required for us to call (for example) a Chihuahua a new species is for it not to be able to breed with a Great Dane. Not a great stretch.

“Why have we never found a transitional fossil?”

This was a really good objection to evolution pointed out a long time ago.

It went like this: If you think one animal evolved into another – fish into amphibians, dinosaurs into birds, monkey ancestors into humans – then you should expect to discover fossils that show this. You should find fossils of fish with legs, dinosaurs with wings, and fossils mid-way between apes and humans.

This is a great point. Science depends on just this kind of objections in order to keep it honest and moving forward.

So, since the objection was raised, scientists have done a lot more digging, and we have now found a whole range of transitional fossils. You can see about 60 of them on Wikipedia. They include fish with legs, dinosaurs with wings, and, yes, a whole range of "missing links" describing the journey from apes to humans.

The transitional fossil argument flew fifty years ago, but now, it's dead and buried. We've been waiting for fifty years for the creationists' next good argument. If you find it, let science know.

“How could a structure like the eye evolve?”

This was another good one fifty years ago.

The eye is a complex structure. If any part of it evolved on its own, it would have been useless. Any tiny change to the structure would have made the creature blind. So how could such a structure just appear out of nowhere?

A good point, and definitely worth investigating. So science investigated it.

We now have a very comprehensive understanding of how eyes developed.

Some creatures skin cells are more sensitive to light than others. Patches of light sensitive cells allowed creatures to detect light and dark – useful in itself. Next, having those cells in a dent in the skin allowed them to detect which direction light came from. Again, a useful adaptation. After that, the more the dent became eyeball shaped, the more focussed the light was and the better the creature could see…. You see where we're going here?

There are living creatures showing all these adaptations from light sensitive cells through to our full eyeball, with each stage offering its own advantages. No need for any jumps or useless half-made organs.

“How come DNA is so complex?

There must have been a creator!”

Imagine you had a massive box of Lego containing building blocks of four colours, red, blue, green and yellow.

Imagine that when you shook the box around, sometimes blocks would randomly fit together, but once fitted they wouldn't come apart.

Now imagine you carried on shaking the box for a million years. Eventually, you'd have millions of blocks fitted together in a massively complex sequence of colors. No intelligence required.

The objection to this might, quite rightly be: "ah, but your colour sequence is random – DNA isn't. It actually does something."

And that's fine, but with the Lego, we haven't added any natural selection. Let's say the red blocks only fitted to the blue ones, and the green ones only fitted to the yellow. Now, when you shook, the result wouldn't be random – you'd get sequences of red and blue blocks, and sequences of green and yellow blocks.

Not random. Not intelligent.

And you could go on. If some combinations could form jaws that broke other blocks apart, they'd come to dominate – the more complicated the environment, the more complex the sequences.

"How can a creature that doesn't have something give rise to one that does?

You can't give what you don't have."

A creature that doesn't have wings can't give its children wings, right?

A creature with arms can give its children longer arms. A creature with fur can give its creature longer, stiffer, more featherlike fur. And slowly, over millions of years, variation can change those arms out of all recognition until they can be used to fly.

A pile of bricks doesn't contain a house, but an arrangement of bricks can certainly become a house.

If the objection to this is, "Ah, but a house needs an architect!" then that's great. That means whoever you're talking to is convinced that DNA can evolve, and now just needs to understand how that can happen naturally due to changes in the environment.

"Why doesn't your brain just believe whatever would be best for its survival?"

If your brain evolved from a monkey-brain just so you could learn how to escape lions on the African grasslands, what makes you think it's up to the job of logical reasoning.

In other words, you can't trust your brain, so trust scripture instead.

A fair enough point, our brains do play a lot of tricks on us. Non believers might say that religion is one of those tricks.

The best way we've found of getting around our brains' natural biases is called science. It requires rigorous testing, and allows anyone on the planet who has a better explanation, or a new test to try it out and contribute to what we know.

It's not perfect, but it's a lot better than just taking the word of one book.

"But you can't
observe evolution,
right?
So you can't know
it's real."

Two problems here.

The first is that we can observe evolution. Check out experiments with fruit flies, selective breeding of farm animals, moths changing colour, viruses mutating. All examples of evolution which we can and have observed.

The second problem is that we don't need to directly observe something to know it's real. We can't see wind, but we can see things blown about by it. We can't see gravity or magnetism, but we can see their effects, and we can measure them, so we know the impact they have in the world.

Likewise, we can observe DNA and see that ours is 98% the same as that of chimps. We can test the results of different portions of the DNA code in different animals, and see how that code has been copied over time. We can dig up fossils and show the progression of traits throughout time, and we can see how ecosystems shape the creatures that live in them.

If science, or religion comes up with a better explanation which fits all this evidence, scientists will have to change their minds. This happens all the time. It's how science works. However, a seven day creation simply does not fit the evidence.

"If you accept things you can't see (e.g. gravity, magnetism, wind), then why not God?"

We can see the effect of gravity on the world. We don't know everything about gravity (or magnetism), but we do know what happens if we drop things.

The same thing happens every time we drop something, and any schoolchild can carry out tests to measure how gravity works, and check their results against our theory of gravity.

If, one day, a schoolchild does that experiment and can get something different to happen, they can write up their experiment and anyone in the world can check it. The child will then collect their Nobel Prize, and we'll have to update the theory of gravity to take account of the new discovery.

If you can show a test that displays any effect your god has on the world that can't be explained better by theories we already have, you too can collect your Nobel Prize, and you'll have added billions of converts to your faith by providing evidence of your god.

If you believe that your god saves the souls of believers, you'll have the eternal life of countless fellow humans to your credit. Why wouldn't you do that?

“Must God be provable by science?”

If anything has an effect on the world, then that effect can be tested and measured.

If you believe in a god which (for example) sometimes cures the sick in response to prayers, then it's a simple matter to test – even if the effect is tiny and very rare.

We just get 1000 sick people, pray for half of them, and don't pray for the other half, then we watch to see who gets better fastest. The effect of God will be right there in the numbers.

In fact, this experiment has been done several times. You can easily find references online. It turns out that prayer has no effect whatsoever.

Try coming up with a similar test for any effect you think your god or gods have on the world.

If, on the other hand, you believe in a non-interventionist god – one who planned out the universe using the laws of physics, then set it into motion to play out as a perfect machine, then that's fine. Such a god wouldn't be provable by science. However, you'd have to ask: what's the difference between such a god and no god at all.

“Can science answer every question?”

No. It can't tell you what color to paint your living room. It can't give you a meaning for your life.

But it can tell you how things happened. It can, and has answered a lot of the questions religion and philosophy have asked in the past. It has, for example, told us why the suns appear to move, and how life appeared. Previously, many Christians have thought that heaven was a physical place in the actual sky and that Hell was somewhere underground. Science can and has disproved this (for most believers). Likewise, we have sent probes towards the Sun, and can be pretty sure it isn't dragged across the sky by winged horses.

Such research is good because it frees up philosophy to explore the questions it's good at. Questions about ethics, and morality, and meaning and purpose. Science can help by informing us about these questions, but it can't answer them on its own.

"Science can explain some things.

The rest are God.."

This argument comes in many forms. "You don't know how the universe began, so it must have been God", "You can't explain consciousness so, God did it", "Quantum physics is a bit odd, so, God.", "You can't show every step on the development of life, so God."

We call this argument "The God of the gaps". Any time there's a gap in knowledge, you can shove a god in there to plug it.

The problem for the faithful is that it's a difficult place to stand. The moment science confirms (for example) that the Earth moves around the Sun rather than the Sun being dragged across the sky by winged horses, religion has to shift to saying that of course, the winged horse thing was just a metaphor. Either that or they have to kill all the scientists.

In other words, you have to keep very up to date on modern science, and be prepared to jump-ship as soon as your particular gap gets closed. If you don't, you can end up looking a little like a flat-earther.

So far, every time science has investigated a gap in its knowledge, religious people have claimed it to be the domain of their god. However, the answer has so far always turned out not to require a god. Despite this, scientists keep looking.

“Science is just another religion.

You worship Darwin (or Satan or Money).”

This crops up a lot, and it comes from the assumption that the religious and non-religious must use the same kind of judgements to reach our conclusions: "You have to accept something as infallible, so if it's not religion, it must be science."

It's tough to get across that this just isn't the case. Nothing about science is infallible. Darwin was wrong about lots of things, Einstein was wrong about lots of things.

The difference between science and religion is that you can check science – and if it's wrong, it has to change.

Science does not expect you to believe or have faith in it. Instead, it provides observations you can check, and tests you can do yourself (if you have the equipment), and it invites you to come up with an alternative theory that explains the results. If you can, science has to change its conclusions.

Religion, on the other hand, does not invite criticism. It claims to be infallible, and will not update with new facts or doctrines.

New science papers are released every day to reflect new things we have observed about the universe. When Bible Version 3 ,4 ,5 , and 6 come out, maybe they'll cover genetics, medicine psychology and astronomy. Until then, we have better sources.

“Where did logic come from?”

Why does the universe make any sense at all, and why, particularly are we able to understand it?

Those are two interesting questions. Sure, you can claim "God did it" as an answer, but that's a little lazy.

There has been a lot of study into this kind of philosophical question, and it gets pretty deep. We can ask, for example, whether logic was invented by humans as a way to make sense of things, or whether it has always been an integral part of the universe, waiting to be discovered.

If you want to do this study, and the person you're talking to wants to do it too, then great. If you don't, then "I don't know, and I don't think you know either" is good enough to be going on with.

"If you're not going to do every experiment in science yourself, then you have to accept the results on faith."

This is the "science is faith" argument again.

If you accept that, for example, "time is relative" – a mad-sounding idea if ever there was one – but you're never prepared to test this (by putting an atomic clock on an aeroplane), then what's the difference between that and faith?

The answer is that you don't have to believe something's true in order to behave as though it is until better evidence comes along. That's pretty much what most of us do most of the time. You aren't asked to "believe" scientific theories, only to treat those with most evidence as a working assumption until a better one comes along.

Every test in science is documented and available to everyone. Lots of people – independent people with no axe to grind – have checked the theory that time is relative. Lots of technology (GPS, for example) depends on the theory working in practice.

By contrast, nobody can check the claim that Christ was resurrected. No experiments are provided in the Koran to verify its claims. Noah left no geographical evidence. That is why we are asked to believe without evidence rather than being offered the opportunity to verify for ourselves.

"Science constantly changes its mind. Why build your beliefs on something that keeps changing?"

It doesn't feel safe, does it, to base your worldview on a moving target?

Religion at least says the same thing today that it said a thousand years ago.

But on the other hand, you wouldn't go to school for years and expect to come out seeing things exactly the same way as you did when you went in. If you did, that would mean you'd learned nothing.

As we learn more about the universe, we're bound to get a different perspective on it, and some of the things we learned before will turn out to be wrong – or at least oversimplified.

The recognition of that fact is what science is based on.

A world-view based on doubt feels less safe than one based on certainty. But certainty means never growing, never learning, and ultimately repeating the same mistakes over and over.

A believer might feel that their scriptures are infallible, so they don't need to learn anything new. Most atheists would find that level of arrogance uncomfortable.

“What would it take to convince you there’s a God?”

For most non-believers, "evidence" would be the answer to this.

Science has one definition for evidence. Law has another, slightly lower bar. No god or gods have so far convinced either a peer-reviewed science journal, or a (sensible) court of law.

Let's clear those barriers then see where we are after that.

"Are you willing to look at the evidence for God?"

Most doubters would be delighted to look at any evidence for anything, and, if that evidence is compelling, most would be prepared to change their minds.

Most non-believers are, after all, on a lifelong and honest search for truth.

You may need to stress, however, that this also means there's a very high bar for what evidence is.

For most people, unsubstantiated quotes from a book – whether that's a science book, or a religious one – aren't evidence. Lots of people all agreeing on something aren't evidence either.

For most people, testimonies of what other people say they've seen, done or felt aren't evidence, and even the evidence of your own eyes and ears is subject to all kinds of mistakes and biases and needs backing up. In fact, even the results of scientific experiments are only evidence until someone comes up with a better experiment.

If this seems impossible, then consider that scientific theory and every court in the land is judged by these standards.

“What about the fulfilled prophecies in the Bible/Koran/other holy book?”

There are two points here.

The first is that it doesn't matter how often something has been right. It only needs to be wrong once. If the law of gravity worked most of the time, but sometimes things went up when you dropped them, you'd know the law was flawed.

If I wrote a list of 10 things on a piece of paper, nine of which were true, would you accept the tenth without other evidence? I hope not. Just because one thing in a document appears true doesn't mean you can take everything else on trust.

The second problem is vagueness and verifiability. If someone is bringing up fulfilled prophecies, then they probably have some in mind. You may or may not have information to hand which would allow you to investigate these prophecies during a conversation. If not, you may want to do that research later if they seem compelling.

On the other hand, many prophecies turn out to be either very vague, or predictive of something that only occurs later in the same book. i.e. saying that someone predicts a messiah will be born in Bethlehem, then, later, someone else claims (without evidence) the person they think is their messiah was born in Bethlehem, that's not evidence of anything.

“How do you explain miracles?”

You could say there are two types of miracles.

First, there are extremely surprising events that don't break the laws of physics, but are incredibly unlikely. Examples include, surviving an aeroplane crash, or having a cancer go into remission spontaneously, or someone getting pregnant when they thought it couldn't happen for them.

The second group are events which break the laws of physics. For example, people flying unaided, or walking on water.

The first group are easy to explain: unlikely things happen all the time. There are eight billion people on the planet, so that's eight billion chances to survive an air crash, recover from a disease or get pregnant.

The second kind of miracle has never been proven to have happened. Not ever. Not once.

We're told by the Bible that in the past, God was continually popping out from behind the clouds to perform undisputed and provable miracles.

However, since everyone got phones with cameras in their pockets, he seems to have given up doing this.

Type "miracles" into YouTube, and you'll find none.

"But I have seen miracles.
I have a personal experience of God.

You can't deny that."

Many people's faith comes down, in the end, to personal experience. They describe the feeling of 'knowing' their god and are able to describe events which are completely convincing to them. These experiences are utterly compelling to them.

But for any religious experience you can name, others have had exactly that experience but been of different faiths or none.

If they were a worshipper of Zeus, they'd feel they had that relationship with Zeus. If they were a Muslim, they would fit it into Islam. It would be exactly the same.

Human brains respond to an imagined relationship in exactly the same way they respond to a real one. The same chemicals are released, and we have the same feelings. Later, when we recall an experience, we make those feelings stronger, and may associate them with prayer, or repeated ritual. We try to make sense of our feelings, and we do so within the framework of whatever we already believe.

You could try asking whether the person having this experience would deny the same experience, or the same miracle if it had happened to someone following, another faith.

You could ask what the knowledge that people with different religions or no religion also experience exactly the same things means to them.

“Why are people willing to die for their beliefs if those beliefs aren’t real?”

People have been committed to a lot of causes throughout history. Some have been good, some bad, some right, some very wrong.

Unfortunately, commitment and belief is no guarantee of anything.

"If you can imagine a perfect god, then one must exist."

This is called the Ontological Argument.

The way it goes is this: You can imagine a perfect being. But if it doesn't exist, then it's not perfect. If it was perfect, then it would exist (since a non-existent being wouldn't be perfect), so if you can imagine it being perfect, then it must exist in order to be perfect.

The problem with this argument is that it's utter nonsense. It depends on appearing complicated and sounding clever. In fact, it's just trying to make something exist by putting the label "existence" into your definition of it.

"A perfect being must exist" so "a perfect being must exist"

Of course, you can say the same about unicorns.

“The Devil did it.”

There are lots of "the devil did it" arguments that get thrown about. Basically, anything that theists see as messing with the minds of non-believers or causing evil in the world can get put down to the devil, or similar beasts.

Obviously not all religious apologists use these arguments, but it's worth understanding them for those who do.

The idea of demons causing mischief in the world is central to some religious ideologies. It allows them to feel that they're in a righteous battle for the soul of the world.

One problem with this is that if you believe in a hell, or a devil, then you have to accept that your God either can't prevent him from doing the things he does, or supports all his actions.

In other words, if there's a devil, then he's on God's side, working for God and with God's full approval – either that or God isn't omnipotent and can't stop him.

For there to be a battle, both sides have to be fallible, otherwise it's not a battle.

"Do you believe Jesus was real, and died for your sins?"

Most historians agree that the Jesus story is based on a real historical figure. There's no physical evidence, so maybe he did live, and maybe he didn't. Either way, he's mentioned by various sources.

As to what he died for, people, throughout history have lived and died for lots of different things. People giving up their lives for their beliefs is often commendable, but not unusual. Nazi soldiers in WWII thought they were sacrificing themselves for the greater good. It doesn't make them right.

Jesus is a great story, but not evidence.

The trick in this question is often the follow up: That some of the same sources that claimed Jesus was real (i.e., the Gospels) also claimed he performed miracles, and rose from the dead -so if you believe he existed, then you have to accept every story told about him.

You don't, of course.

Most historians accept that what we call the Gospels were originally written years after the events they describe, and passed from person to person before being written down.

About 100 years later, the Church Fathers simply decided to say they were written by Matthew, Mark, Luke and John.

“How can you be moral without God?”

If you don't believe in God, then all morality that exists is without God. Everyone who is moral is moral without God.

But the real point of the question is to ask where your ethical code comes from. For a religious person, the answer is simple. It comes from their infallible god.

The problem with having an ethical code which comes from somewhere you claim is infallible is that there's a temptation to not take responsibility when it turns out that code leads you to do bad things. You can just say "it's God's will" and carry right on with slavery, persecution or genocide without feeling you even have to understand why you're doing it.

For a non-believer, it's a tougher question. It's likely there will be a number of sources and ideas you think about when trying to decide what's right. It's likely some of those sources will be things you've seen, things you've learned, and some may even be religious teachings that have struck a chord with you.

It's not easy to put this into words – to explain your exact set of complex references, which will change as you grow – and you don't need to.

It's likely your ethical values will be pretty similar to those of the person you're talking to on some level. Try asking them if it's really only the fear of God that stops them becoming a murderer. If it's not, then there's your answer. God is irrelevant to morality.

“Is it always wrong to kill babies?

Do you believe in evil?

There's a logical train of thought behind this question, and it's often used in various forms.

The point is that if you believe anything is always wrong, then that must mean there's an idea of right and wrong that comes from outside your own mind. In other words, a supernatural set of ethical rules that exist separate from ourselves.

There are certainly things that all (or most) humans consider wrong. However, the universe shows no sign of agreeing with us. Everyone thinks killing babies is wrong, but malaria doesn't think that. Neither do crocodiles.

Our morality is something we have evolved to help our species survive (a species which kills its own babies isn't going to survive very long). It's vitally important, but it exists only within us, and it's up to us to imprint it into the world.

On the plus side, this means every morally good thing that ever happened, happened because we've made it happen.

"If there is law,
then surely there's
a lawmaker?"

Again – there's no evidence for any moral law, or fairness in the universe except fairness created by humans. Humans are the only law makers.

Not all of the unfairness in the world is down to humans, but all of the fairness is.

Fairness is something we've created, and if you look at the history of the world, it's a story of faltering movement towards a fairer world.

Many non-religious people see the human story not as a negative story of fall from grace, but as the positive story of a rise from chaos.

“Does life have any meaning or purpose?”

Wouldn't it be dull if everyone had the same meaning or purpose?

The good news is that if there's no god, then everyone gets to choose their own.

One person's purpose may be to help those in need. Another person may see their purpose as learning and understanding. Still another may find meaning in family, or friends, nature, or culture.

Some people find a meaning or purpose in their religion, and that's fine. Just because non-believers find it elsewhere, doesn't negate the contribution of the religious.

The huge range of things in which we find meaning as humans is one reason why we have such an amazing world.

"Do you believe in free will?"

This question gets asked usually to raise the idea that a god has created us, but given us all freedom of choice so we can decide how to live our lives. That way the god isn't responsible for the actions of its creations, and gets to judge us for not obeying whatever rules it's set us. It's a way to dodge the obvious bullet that if a perfect god created the universe, then our behaviour, including all "sin" and including your lack of belief in him, must all be part of his plan and must originate with him.

However, we do know a lot more about what drives our decisions than we knew when the Bible was written.

We know, for example, that free will is affected by genetics, by environment, and by experiences we've had. A lion and a lamb both have free will, but if you put them in a field together, they will choose to express that free will in very predictable ways. Free choice depends on who you are.

A god would have to choose our tendencies and weaknesses and if it were "perfect" then it would still know exactly what it would take to cause that me to make choices. If you doubt this, then ask yourself whether, when, the first time you heard the Genesis story, you instinctively knew Adam and Eve would eat the apple. If you did, congratulations, you have a better understanding of human free will than God.

“Aren’t the laws of religion a good ethical code?”

Most non-believers would probably agree that a lot of the lessons that religion teaches are pretty good ones. However:

1) You can probably think of some religious rules that are either utterly pointless or just plain horrid.
2) Religion didn't create any of the moral codes it claims. People thought murder and theft were wrong a long time before the Bible told them so, and those that wanted to kill and steal carried right on after the Bible.
3) An ethical code, however great it is, does not suggest the existence of a creator. There are good natural reasons why social animals develop rules by which to run their societies. Wolves would not survive if they ate their own pack.
4) A set of rules that doesn't develop as we learn more about the world risks forcing increasingly bad decisions as it becomes more out of date. Stoning someone for adultery, for example, seems a little OTT these days, and religious texts that don't reference science often break down when applied to modern healthcare.
5) Without god, you can agree on the best rules from all sources.

"Why is there love?"

Humans evolved on the African savanna. But we're slow moving, weak, and not well camouflaged.

However, we had one key advantage. We were sociable. We cared for each other, and we worked together.

People often think survival of the fittest means survival of the fastest, the meanest, the most selfish. But often, that isn't the case. Teamwork beats individual strength in animals from fish to bees to buffalo.

And by caring for our young for longer than most animals, we allowed them time to learn complex social skills, and intelligence so caring became our survival strategy.

In the case of humans, survival of the fittest meant survival of the closest group, the most compassionate family. Survival of the strongest love.

"You can't prove love. Does that mean you don't believe in it?"

You can prove love. Everything people do and say when they are in love is evidence of love.

Of course love is defined by the people feeling it, and exists in their minds alone, so it's certainly possible to be wrong about it, or to have a different definition of it from the person you love.

That doesn't mean your feelings aren't real.

If the purpose of this question is to compare belief in love to belief in a god, then it makes the non believers' point quite well:

Love is an idea in the mind, and your feelings about it are real. It can make you perform actions in the real world, but it can't do anything without your input. Love can't go out and buy your partner flowers. You have to do it on love's behalf. Nobody pretends that love is a physical being – it's just an idea.

The same is true about God. It's an idea in your mind, and while your feelings about it are real, and those feelings can make you do things, there's no reason to see it as a physical being outside of your mind.

“Is the world getting worse?”

It's quite a common tactic when someone is trying to convert you, for them to paint a despondent and frightening picture of the world.

You could, if you were feeling cynical, take that as confirmation that few people ever find religion when they're already happy.

This point of view often displays a quite negative view of humanity. Humans are seen as sinful, degraded creatures spiralling towards the apocalypse, whose only hope is to be rescued by an external supernatural force (God).

Atheists are free to embrace a different view. That of a human creature which has risen from humble origins among the other life with which we share our world, and which, century on century has carved out growing civilisation with understanding, compassion and science. A creature which is both flawed, and blessed by evolutionary gifts which have allowed us to double our lifespans, reduce disease, poverty and ignorance, and which allow us to probe the deepest questions of existence.

Of course, it's certainly possible to be religion-free and still be pessimistic or ambivalent about the future, but without gods, we do at least hold that future in our own hands.

“Why do so many people believe?”

Though atheists are fond of saying "nobody is born believing in a god - we're all atheists until people start lying to us" this is a bit disingenuous.

In fact, humans have been inventing Gods as far back as we have been able to trace human behaviour. We've done it in every culture, and in every society since we first started painting on walls and carving mammoth bones. Why we do that is a good question, and we shouldn't dismiss it out of hand.

As humans we're a curious bunch. We can't look at anything for long without wanting to know how it works. This curiosity has been our special survival skill since we first evolved - that and our ability to form social bonds by using shared stories to help us work together.

Being curious basically means spotting patterns and telling stories about them. We saw vultures circling and told the story that this pointed the way to fresh meat. We saw the changing colours of trees and reminded ourselves of the story that this meant fruit would soon be ripe.

As we became cleverer, this search for patterns enabled us to create tools, and art. But it also deceived us. When we looked at the stars, we couldn't help but attempt to read our fortunes in them. When we saw the changing seasons we couldn't help but read magical spirits into them. When we saw the wonder of life and death, our brains forced us to see the hand of a creator who wasn't really there.

Accepting that some things are just random is something that human brains simply aren't equipped to do.

"Wouldn't you rather believe in a God than in nothing?"

Most non-believers have worked hard to get past the natural human tendency to believe what you would like to be true rather than what the evidence, or lack of evidence shows. It's not helpful to consider what you'd *like* to be true when trying to work out what *is* true.

We don't say to someone standing on top of a tall building, "Wouldn't you rather believe you could fly?" We don't react to the news of a doctor's diagnosis with "Ah, but I'd rather I was well" (or, at least, we don't expect that to help). A scientist doesn't object to a rebuttal of their research paper with "Yes, but I'd rather I was right"

What we'd rather believe in is not important.

"Trust me / Don't trust non-believers/scientists/ etc."

Scientists never try to win an argument based on who or what to trust.

Deciding whether something is true should never be done based on what you think of the person who said it. In science, this means that every single claim made has to come with a set of evidence or tests you can check out yourself (assuming you have the time and equipment).

If someone is a believer in something, or being paid by someone you don't agree with, and they make a claim, then it's good practice to check out carefully whether their evidence stacks up before you dismiss it. If someone you agree with or believe in makes a claim, then exactly the same rules apply.

Trust has absolutely nothing to do with it.

"Do you live according to your beliefs?"

This question is generally a sign that you're speaking to someone with whom you can have a genuine honest conversation. For many religious people, how you "live" your faith is the central aspect of it (rather than whether it's based on objective truth or not). This makes perfect sense. Probably most atheists and religious people alike would agree that what you do in this life is more important than what you believe or don't believe about it.

For some non-believers, this is a difficult question, though, because not believing in something isn't actually a belief, and doesn't, in itself, provide a list of rules to live by. For many non-believers, their non-belief is completely separate from their sense of right and wrong. It also brings up a confusion between two meanings of the word "belief":

If you believe in unicorns, then you're saying you think unicorns are a real part of the physical universe - they exist. If you believe in truth, or justice, you're not saying that truth and justice are physical beings. You're saying that you're going to do your best through the force of your actions to make them exist for yourself and the people you care about.

You could see religion as the confusion of these two meanings - the idea that if you want something to be true, then you can make it physically true.

It might be worth being clear about what kind of beliefs you're talking about before you fall into the linguistic trap of listing your approach to them.

"What happens when you die?

What about your soul?"

The ultimate "nobody knows" question.

Nobody dead has provably returned to life. It can be difficult to get past talk of either (a) the claims of Jesus' resurrection and (b) near death experiences.

However, if you don't accept either, you can still have a fruitful discussion.

Disbelief in life after death is often associated with atheism, but they are not necessarily the same thing.

Gods aren't necessary for belief in life after death (although they provide some easy answers). Many Buddhists, Panpsychists, and other believers in a spiritual world are also atheists.

But it's also perfectly reasonable to say either that nobody can possibly have a clue, or that consciousness seems to be purely a result of electrical signals in the brain which cease when you're dead.

Lots of questions arise from any position you take, and so they should.

"You've got one life that you know of. Live it well" seems to be a starting point which most people, religious or not, can agree on.

"How do you know your reasoning is working correctly?"

It's a fair enough question. If we're creatures who have evolved to scavenge on the African savanna, why would we imagine we can tackle the existential questions of life and death?

The answer is that our reasoning is frequently wrong. One example of its wrongness is our willingness to believe in supernatural forces without evidence.

Our best shot so far at overcoming the limitations of our minds is to create tests and observations which can be checked in lots of different ways by everyone else in the world and are able to be constantly criticised and updated as people with different perspectives find things wrong with them.

We call this science.

"Why do you deny God?"

The word "deny" is the problem here. It contains within it the assumption that God exists, and you know it. Your "denial" is dishonest.

If you don't believe in god or gods, then there's nothing to deny. A Christian, for example, doesn't need to deny Zeus. With no evidence that Zeus exists, the Christian can just ignore Zeus and put any reference to him down as a made up story.

You might suggest that the question is rephrased along the lines of:

"Why don't you have the same exact set of views as I do, and believe in the same one of the ten thousand odd deities humanity has invented that I worship?"

This phrasing might help create a more even-handed dialogue, and also has the advantage that it pretty much answers itself.

If they don't like that rephrasing, maybe they can suggest some form of the question that you can both agree on.

“You just want to sin!”

This is a tricky one because, for many, the trigger that leads them to re-examine their faith is the realisation that it's not compatible with their own ethical standards or principles.

The fact that religion defines something as a sin when it turns out to be nothing of the kind that can make you re-think your faith. And, if you were going to change nothing about your behaviour, following your de-conversion, what would be the point of it?

But this is actually a red herring. It's not the trigger that matters, it's what it leads you to realise. A doctor examining a patient because of one symptom might find a whole range of things wrong with them that need treating.

You might not want to discuss what made you look again at your faith, and you don't have to. What made you doubt faith, presumably, was a lack of belief in a god. Sin or no sin, that question is the one that needs an answer. Turn the question back to one of evidence.

If your interrogator persists, point out that if you just wanted to sin, there's an established route used by many people in every church. They just remain and sin secretly, then they repent if discovered, and carry on. It's much easier.

Would that be more honest?

“Why do you hate God?”

Hate gets mentioned quite often in conversations about faith. It's worth defusing it at source early on to set the ground-rules for a compassionate exchange.

You can't hate something you don't believe in.

Mentioning hatred of god here is an attempt to move the ground of the discussion away from the flaws of religion and onto an infallible god.

If you have a disagreement with religion or religious practice, then be clear that this is your target. Stick doggedly to that target. The distraction of hatred of god is just that.

It's quite possible that the person you're talking to will be able to agree with you that some moments in the history of their religion have not lived up to the standards their ideals have set them.

“Why did you stop believing?”

Did something bad happen to you to make you renounce faith?”

This seems, on the face of it to be an honest question, and it may be intended as one.

However, the effect is to turn the conversation from a dialogue about faith to an examination of your character. This raises the stakes for you, because it's now about discovering what's wrong with you – allowing you to be pushed into areas you may find difficult. At the same time, it lowers the stakes for the other person, allowing them to avoid difficult questions about the faith itself.

The implication is that moving away from religion is something you've done because of some issue you have – rather than because you've found problems with religion itself.

Feel free to follow into this area if you feel comfortable doing so, but recognise that it's a (probably unconscious) attempt to put you on the defensive and avoid tackling the issues you want to explore.

"There's no such thing as an atheist!

You know in your heart that God is real."

There are two different fronts to this one.

The first is the (incorrect) assumption that atheism is the belief that gods don't exist. Because nobody can prove the non-existence of God, so the argument goes, nobody can truly be an atheist.

It's wrong, of course, firstly because people can believe anything they like – and some definitely do believe they can prove the non-existence of gods. And secondly, it's wrong because atheism doesn't mean that. It's non-belief, not a belief in non-existence.

The second argument here is more aggressive: There's no such thing as an atheist because everyone "knows in their heart" that whatever god your challenger is talking about is real.

This is a bad one. They're basically saying you're lying about not believing. Whilst this can come from a simple conviction that they can see the work of their god in everything around them, so you must be able to as well, it's still a problem.

Your job now is not to convince them that you're right. It's to make them understand that you honestly and sincerely believe that you're right, and you're seeking truth just as they are. If you can do that, you have done the world a great service.

“Atheists are evil. Just look at Hitler, Stalin, etc.”

There are a few ways to tackle this.

Sure, there are bad non-believers - but you can probably think of 10x as many bad religious people.

But this is a bad road. You'll end up naming evildoers on both sides - and the non-believer can be pretty confident that we can list religiously motivated evils well into the night while the apologist will run out after about 4 obvious atheist ones.

However, you'll likely end up in an off-topic discussion of whether religious killers kill in the name of their religion, whilst atheists tend not to kill for atheism, but for politics, or of what relationship the (catholic-raised) Hitler had with his god, or of the extent to which antisemitism is driven by religious motives or racial ones. You could play 'atrocity bingo" all night but that may not help. It's essentially an argument that continually raises the stakes.

A kinder answer might be that there are more religious atrocities because religion has always been in power. So when you see an atheist's apparent anger against religion, its worth seeing that from their point of view, they're often fighting against oppressive power.

“Atheism requires faith.”

This is back to a misunderstanding. There's the assumption here that you don't just not believe in a god or gods, but you actively believe they're not real.

Unless you can get the person you're speaking with to accept this, you won't get far.

Try:

"If I told you I had a pet elephant, you could just believe me without proof, or you could believe that I was lying – again without proof. Both would require faith.

A third option would be to simply ask me to prove it. That wouldn't need any faith, and you could live your life as though I didn't have an elephant until I turned up with my elephant.

In addition, whether I turned out to have an elephant or not, it would still have been reasonable of you to demand proof."

Or,

"Do you need faith to not believe in Thor?"

Or simply,

"What do you think atheism means?"

“You just want to get rid of religion!”

Most non-believers are not trying to get rid of religion. Nobody has all the answers, and a range of beliefs, views and perspectives makes the world more colorful and keeps all world views moving forwards.

Most non-believers would be happy for other people to believe whatever they like as long as those beliefs don't adversely affect others.

Many do, however, see the power religion holds in various societies, and the abuses committed by it as a problem. As those religions become less popular (and religion is becoming less popular the world over), many feel that religion will need to take less of a role in society.

It's natural, then, that religious people feel threatened by non-belief. After all, if you truly believe that your faith holds the knowledge of how life should be lived, it's a terrifying thought that your influence may be shrinking, and it's easy to react aggressively in response.

It's worth understanding aggression from the religious for what it is – fear – and doing your best to reduce that fear by assuring your companions that you share many ethical standards.

"Why don't you ever doubt your doubts?"

Most non-believers doubt their doubts all the time.

Doubting is pretty much what not believing is all about. When you doubt, you are curious, you are inquiring, you are open to learning. Doubt is a constant lifelong creative process.

Again this question could be an indication the person you're speaking with hasn't grasped the difference between not believing in something and having an unsupported belief that it doesn't exist.

It's certainty that's the enemy here. As soon as you're certain about anything (including the non-existence of anything) you're not open to new evidence. You stop learning.

Again, show me the evidence, and I'll be happy to readjust my views.

"Why do non-believers go on about God so much?"

God or gods may not exist, but religion definitely exists, and it has a lot of power.

Mention religions which your companions don't believe in, and they'll probably agree that those religions have too much power.

If they do, try mentioning abuses created by their religion, and see if you can get them to see the harm its power over people has had in the past. From there, you can explore what current influence religion has, and how it can negatively affect people who don't believe.

If you are prepared to mention times when you personally have experienced, or felt the oppressive force of religion in your life, this will probably help.

However, regardless, saying non-believers shouldn't talk about religion is like saying people threatened by fascism shouldn't talk about fascism.

"How can you dismiss my religion if you haven't read the Bible/Koran/this or that holy book/fully understood my culture?"

You don't need to know everything about a belief system to know you don't want to be a part of it.

If you've never read Mein Kampf, you can still be against fascism. You don't need a degree in Greek mythology to say that Zeus isn't evidenced.

If you don't believe in any gods, then it's likely you give all of them the same status – that of stories which some people believe, but you don't.

You may feel you'd need a lot more evidence than you've currently seen before you'd move, for example, the Koran to the top of your reading list.

That's perfectly justifiable. You can't read everything. You have to prioritise, and if someone wants you to prioritise their book, they have to convince you they deserve a place along-side all the other authors you want to read.

In any case, if it is discovered that a holy book contains definitive proof of the existence of a god, you'll hear about it pretty quickly on the news, in the scientific journals, and in the Nobel Prize list.

“Satan is lying to you!”

This is a way to avoid listening to what you have to say.

As soon as someone claims your words are the words of some demon, they can feel secure in ignoring everything you have to say even if it makes perfect sense to them.

This is a last refuge argument. It's basically admitting they can't refute what you've said, so they have to invoke some magical deception.

That may be a compliment to your eloquence, but it doesn't help you find common ground.

Try asking how they can tell the difference between Satan's voice and the voice of reason.

Try asking what convinced them that Satan was at work in the world. Moving them back to their own experience will make them feel more secure and positive.

In the end, a person convinced that yours is the voice of the Devil will probably want to end your conversation quickly. This is probably no bad thing.

"I'll pray for you."

This usually comes at the end of a conversation, and is used as a way for the believer to bow out gracefully.

It can feel like a patronising attempt to shut down any further questions and get the last word. You can probably think of a dozen glib comebacks.

However, it probably isn't meant in any but the kindest way, and you're best off taking it on face value.

Think of it this way:

By saying "I'll pray for you", they are accepting that they, themselves can't adequately answer the points you've raised. If they knew what to say to you, they'd say it. Instead, they're recognising that they need to go away and ask a higher authority to answer your questions.

"I'll pray for you" is the religious equivalent of "I'll go and ask my supervisor".

You can see it as an indication that you've made a strong point, and, if the person you're talking to is serious, they are agreeing to think about what you've said during their prayers.

That's as much as you can expect of anyone.

"God loves you."

This is a slightly vaguer version of "I'll pray for you". Again, it's used as a conversation stopper, or at least a punctuation to change the subject.

However, unlike "I'll pray for you", this variant doesn't commit your companion to taking away any homework from the conversation.

Something you've said may have caused them to pause, and certainly, if they could think of a reply to answer your point, you'd have heard it by now, rather than this platitude.

They may mean it. They may even be prepared to consider more deeply something you've said, but they're not prepared to commit to doing so.

"The Lord works in mysterious ways."

This is a catch-all phrase, and there are many variants. "We cannot know the mind of God", "It will all become clear in the fullness of time", "Some things are meant/not meant to be".

The problem with it is that if you're going to base your morality on a being whose ethics you can't understand, that means you can never trust your own judgement about what's right or wrong.

This, in turn, means you risk accepting some interpretation of a religious leader, or a holy scripture even when it contradicts what you believe to be right. If you're willing to accept "God's law" even when it seems immoral, you're on shaky ground.

When you're told that your god punishes gay people, or condones slavery, you just have to accept that your god must have his reasons. Your own truth is subservient.

In addition, this argument would work just as well in defending any kind of god. If you believed in an evil god, you could write off any good you saw in the world with exactly the same line.

“I don’t have enough faith to be an atheist.”

The idea here is to cast non-belief as a belief in itself.

It's usually followed by a list of things that non-believers would have to believe about the universe, or the Bible, or life in general in order to sustain their lack of belief.

But people who aren't convinced by a religion don't need an alternative belief. They only need questions.

It's absolutely ok not to know the answers to those questions (in fact, many would argue, it's the most rational position). If you're not convinced, you're not convinced. Why you're not convinced is up to you.

Nobody can tell you what you have to believe.

And no faith is required to not believe in something.

"You are being tested."

It's a cheap shot to dismiss any questions anyone has as simply the tests of their god. The implication is that you pass the test by ignoring the questions, or at least by finding answers that would be acceptable within whatever religion you find yourself.

Often, this line comes as a response to something that has happened to you to make you question your faith. What you're being told here is that your questions aren't valid. You just need to get over whatever it is, and carry on.

This is unlikely to work.

The other problem with the sentiment is that if you believe in an omnipotent god, then they'd already know how you'd react in any situation. Even if you have free will, an omnipotent being would be able to predict exactly your responses to every test.

A test is only needed if you don't know what the result is going to be. If you're omnipotent, you know, so tests are pointless for an all powerful god.

Some believers, however, mean something else by "being tested" – they mean being given an experience that leads to a strengthening of character. If someone wants to look at life that way, that's fine. But it does mean that if your response to the "test" is a rejection of faith, then you haven't failed. You've grown.

“Atheists are arrogant.”

This one has come out of some robust statements from atheists which have been seen as ridiculing and attacking religion.

In those atheists' defence, scientists take exactly this tone in robust discussions with each other all the time, and they do it without malice, and in the full expectation that people with the opposing view will come back with equally strong arguments, and force them to rethink their position. It is only by both sides putting their positions in as watertight and clinical manner as they can that strong conclusions can be reached.

Unfortunately, religious entrants into such debates are not often versed in such rigorous argument, so their responses are often loud, but fairly flawed, so it can come across a little like kicking a puppy.

You might be tempted to point out that church leaders doling out infallible proclamations while sitting on golden thrones wearing crowns they've made for themselves should probably think twice before using the word "arrogant". After all, atheists are rarely sent out into the world to "save" the unconverted, or demand unelected access to political power.

However, the best way to stop yourself from being called arrogant remains avoiding being arrogant.

Be gentle, be humble, and be aware of how your language will be perceived. After all, we are all on a journey.

Part III

Printed in Dunstable, United Kingdom

76459934R00131